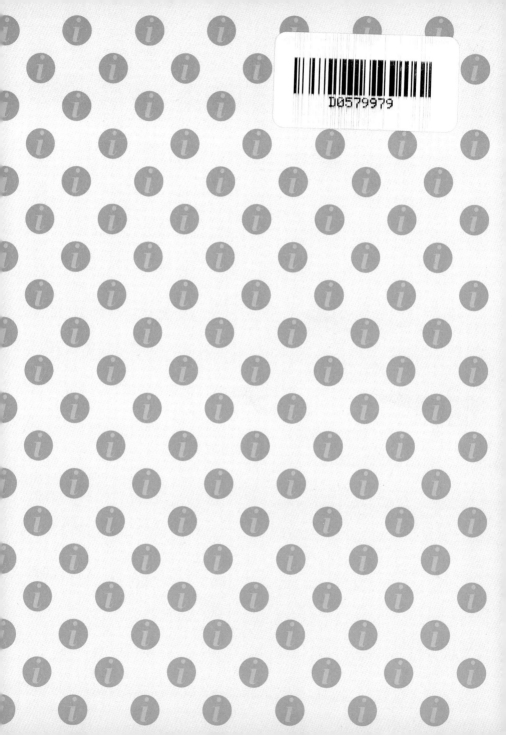

FRESHWATER AQUARIUM FISH

The new compact study guide and identifier

FRESHWATER
AQUARIUM FISH

The new compact study guide and identifier

Derek J. Lambert

CHARTWELL
BOOKS, INC.

A QUINTET BOOK
Published by Chartwell Books
A Division of Book Sales, Inc.
114 Northfield Avenue
Edison, New Jersey 08837

This edition produced for sale
in the U.S.A., its territories
and dependencies only.

ISBN-0-7858-0867-1

This book was designed and produced by
Quintet Publishing Limited
6 Blundell Street
London N7 9BH

Creative Director: Richard Dewing
Art Director: Silke Braun
Designer: James Lawrence
Project Editor: Diana Steedman
Editor: John Wright

Typeset in Great Britain by
Central Southern Typesetters, Eastbourne
Manufactured in Singapore by
Bright Arts (Singapore) Pte Ltd.
Printed in Singapore by
Star Standard Industries (Pte) Ltd.

CONTENTS

INTRODUCTION

The hobby of aquarium fish-keeping has a long history, probably stretching back over 300 years. Originally only native species were kept, but there are reports of goldfish (*Carassius auratus*) reaching Europe as early as 1611 and the first tropical species, the paradise fish – (*Macropodus opercularis*) arrived in 1869. Ornamental fish-keeping and breeding, however, started long before this. In ancient Chinese records, there are reports of colored goldfish having been found as early as A.D. 265 and that serious breeding began about A.D. 800. Poetry of this period even mentions the goldfish, so they must have been widespread and popular at this time.

ABOVE: The Paradise Fish (Macropodus opercularis) *was the first tropical fish to be introduced to the hobby in 1869. Undoubtedly its tolerance to low temperatures helped it survive the rudimentary conditions.*

**A PURELY DIAGRAMMATIC FISH TO SHOW
THE POSITION OF VARIOUS FINS AND BODY PARTS**

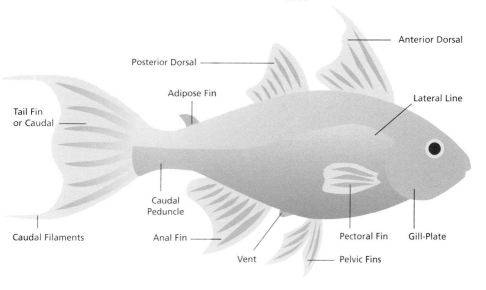

WHAT IS A FISH?

A fish can be defined as any cold-blooded, legless, aquatic organism which possesses a backbone, gills, and at least a median fin as well as a tail. Of the animals which this definition includes, two classes compose what most people think of as fish. These are Chrondrichthyes (sharks and rays), which have a cartilaginous skeleton, and Osteichthyes, which are the bony fish. Despite both these classes also having well-developed gill arches, a pair of pectoral fins, and a pair of pelvic fins, some scientists say only the bony fish should be considered as true fish.

Even if you only include the bony fish, there are over 25,000 species of fish in the world that have adapted to live in almost every aquatic habitat, from the deepest oceans to the shallowest streams. You can even find fish in the most unlikely of habitats. In underground rivers, they have adapted to life without light and survive on only the most minimal amounts of food. In ponds and rivers which dry up during the dry season, the fish have to dig themselves a burrow in the mud and hibernate for many months or lay eggs in the substrate which hatch out when the rains come.

MOVING AROUND

Fish move in a variety of ways and use each fin in a very specific way to generate motion. The most common method is to move the caudal fin from side to side to generate forward motion, but this is more often used when the fish wants a sudden burst of speed or is fighting against a current. The rest of the time, the pectoral fins are often employed. These much smaller fins are positioned on each side of the body behind the gill plates and move the fish around in a much more gentle fashion using less energy than the caudal fin.

Some fish have unusual body shapes or fins and employ different methods to move around. Knifefish have a small or thread-like dorsal fin, but the anal fin is extended along almost the whole length of the body. This undulates in a similar way to a snake and produces forward or backward motion as the fish desires. Mudskippers have developed very strong pectoral fins which enable them to hold their body up and "walk" over land. Other fish will jump clear out of the water to reach flying insects or escape danger, and some will even haul themselves out of a pond or river and then slither like a snake through the damp grass to reach a different habitat. Several predatory fish find this a very useful talent!

DIETARY REQUIREMENTS

It would be very easy if all fish ate the same diet and all we aquarists had to do was put a pinch of flake food in the tank a couple of times a day. The fact is that every species of fish has evolved in a specific way to eat certain types of food. Some feed primarily on vegetable matter while others are predators which eat only live foods, such as insects or fish. There are even specialist feeders which eat only the scales or eyes of other fish.

While such specialist feeders are not generally kept in the aquarium, a wide variety of fish species are, and no one food will be sufficient to keep them all

happy. Commercial foods are formulated to provide a good diet for the majority of commonly kept aquarium fish. These should form the basis of your fishes' diet, but you still need to feed other foods as well.

Live foods of various types can be purchased at most aquarium shops and should be fed to your fish once a week. Failing this you can use the frozen equivalents if live foods are unavailable at certain times of year. As an occasional substitute for live food, it does not really matter whether it is frozen blood-worms or black mosquito larvae. If it is going to be several months before live foods are available again (during harsh

ABOVE LEFT: Archer Fish (Toxotes opercularis) *use their caudal fin to generate sudden bursts of forward motion which enable them to jump clear of the water to catch low-flying insects.*

RIGHT: The Checker Barb (Barbus oligolepis) *is a typical omnivore, eating all kinds of food.*

winters this is often the case), then you must buy several types and feed them in rotation.

If you have fish that feed primarily on vegetable matter, you should buy a herbivore food and feed this from time to time instead of the normal flake food. Blanched lettuce leaves, boiled potato, and liquidized spinach are also good foods for these fish and should be fed every week.

Predators, on the other hand, should be fed with a carnivore food if they will eat it. If they are reluctant to eat commercial flake or granulated foods, try them on pieces of fish and if that fails, various live foods such as blood-worms, *Daphnia* or, for large fish,

earthworms. Some species, however, only eat live fish and must be fed these. Feeder fish are often found for sale in aquarium shops at a very cheap price. If you are thinking of having a predator like this, make sure you can afford to keep it and can secure a supply of food for it. (Some shops refuse to sell 20 Neon Tetras per week to a customer once they know they are food for another fish.)

REPRODUCTION IN FISH
From the very earliest days, it has not just been the lovely colors and graceful movement of aquarium fish that has captured aquarists' interest but the fascinating breeding habits of many

ABOVE: The female Lindu Duckbill (Xenopoecilus sarasorium) *has been carrying her eggs for 15 days. This method of brood care increases the embryo's chance of survival.*

species. Some people think all fish scatter their eggs over the gravel or in plants and that is the last the adults have to do with them. Aquarists, however, have found this is far from the truth for many species. While lots of fish do just scatter their eggs and swim away, others try to protect them from predators. The humble stickleback (*Gasterosteus aculeatus*), which children catch in their local park pond, builds a nest from plant material on the bottom and guards the eggs and young. Other species, such as the honey gourami (*Colisa chuna*), build a nest of bubbles at the water's surface and place their eggs in this. The male guards the nest until the young are able to fend for themselves.

Other species of fish go even further to protect their eggs by holding them in their mouth until they hatch. Quite a number of cichlids, gouramis, and some snakeheads use this method. Other species site their eggs on different parts of their body. Some species of catfish hold them on their lower lip, pipefish place them in a pouch on the male's stomach, while *Xenopoecilus sarasorium* have them hanging down from the female's vent on a thread like a bunch of grapes. All these methods increase the chance that the eggs will survive until they hatch.

One group of fish, however, make certain of this by holding the eggs inside their body until they are ready to

ABOVE: The One-sided Livebearer (Jenynsia lineata) *carries its young inside its body for up to eight weeks before giving birth to large, robust fry.*

hatch and then giving birth to free-swimming babies. These are the live-bearers which are very often the first species of fish an aquarist will breed. As a group they are very diverse. Most aquarists know them as four of the most popular aquarium fish: guppies, platies, mollies, and swordtails. These are only a small fraction of the fish that bear their young alive as a reproductive method. There are livebearers from every part of the world. In Russia livebearing fish live in deep-water lakes. The seas teem with livebearing fish, such as stingrays and many of the sharks.

FISH CONSERVATION

Freshwater fish are disappearing from the wild at an alarming rate, and un-fortunately not very much is being done to stop their decline. In 1979 the American Fisheries Society produced a list of endangered and threatened fishes in the USA, Canada, and Mexico. This list was horrific enough with 251 species listed, but in 1989 a new list was produced which contained 364 species of fish needing protection because of their rarity. This is a staggering increase in just 10 years and gives you an idea of the scale of the problem.

The situation in the rest of the world is every bit as bad. Indeed there are now thousands of fish in trouble in the wild, and many of these have traditionally been popular aquarium fish. The 1994 I.U.C.N. (The World Conservation Union) Red List of threatened animals includes fish such as the cherry barb (*Barbus titteya*) and Celebes rainbow (*Telmatherina ladigesi*). Both are staples of the aquarium hobby being bred by the thousands on commercial fish farms. In the vast majority of cases (if not all), it is triple evils of habitat de-struction, pollution, and exotic species introductions which have caused the decline in native fish populations.

Many scientists and conservationists have now come to the conclusion that captive breeding of fish is the only way many species are going to survive in the future, and it is clear that aquarists have a very important role to play in this. Even with all the zoos and public aquariums working together to main-tain only those species already on the endangered lists, there are not enough resources to look after them all. Most people involved in endangered species protection work firmly expect the lists to more than double in the next 10 years. It is obvious that only by involving the millions of aquarists around the world are we going to save these fish from extinction.

HOW TO USE THIS BOOK

This book attempts to provide as much information as possible, on a wide variety of aquarium fish, in a clear and easily understood way. The species have been arranged into fish families or suborders with the species listed alphabetically (by scientific name) within each group.
Under species headings the information has been divided into a brief description, the distribution of the fish in the wild, and its temperament and care in captivity. Some details of how a particular fish breeds is also given and four "at a glance" symbols indicate the species suitability for a community aquarium, dietary requirements, area of the aquarium it occupies, and the temperature range needed for its well being.

KEY TO SYMBOLS

Community

Yes    No

Dietary requirements

Carnivore    Omnivore    Herbivore

Area of aquarium

Surface    Midwater    Bottom

Temperature

79°f
▲
70°f

Carp-like fish

SUBORDER *Cyprinoidei*

This suborder of fish contains many of the very popular

aquarium fish, including barbs, danios, loaches, rasboras, and the

most popular aquarium fish in the world – goldfish. They have a

single dorsal fin usually situated midway down the body, and there are

no proper spines in the fins. They vary in size from fish which are

fully grown at just over 1 inch to those measuring about 5 feet.

Most members of this suborder are omnivores

and will eat all types of food. Some have barbels which they use to

grub around in the substrate searching for food, while others are

primarily midwater fish that take food in the water column

before it reaches the bottom.

SILVER SHARK *BALANTIOCHEILUS MELANOPTERUS*

DESCRIPTION The silver shark is covered with large silver scales that look like a polished mirror. The fins are silver to yellowish with bold black edges. It has a long streamlined body and can grow up to 1 ft.

DISTRIBUTION Southeast Asia.

TEMPERAMENT & CARE Despite being a large species, this fish is peaceful and will fit in well with other community fish. Due to its large size, it can only be kept in an aquarium which is at least 6½ ft. long and 1½ ft. wide.

79°f
▲
70°f

BREEDING Thought to be an egg-scatterer in common with other closely related fish.

CHECKER BARB *BARBUS OLIGOLEPIS*

DESCRIPTION A small barb species reaching a maximum size of just over 1½ in. As young fish they only have a faint, black, reticulated pattern to the body and a few black blotches along the flanks. Adult males have red fins edged in black.

DISTRIBUTION Indonesia and Sumatra.

TEMPERAMENT & CARE A peaceful, lively, shoaling species which is perfect for the community tank. Eats all foods and adapts well to most conditions.

BREEDING Egg-scatterer which spawns at first light. Males will choose a particular plant as the center of their territory and entice ripe females to spawn there. Once they have finished, the adults will devour all the eggs they can find.

79°f
▲
70°f

TINFOIL BARB *BARBUS SCHWANEFELDI*

81°f
▲
70°f

DESCRIPTION A deep-bodied, diamond-shaped fish which at 14 in. is one of the larger barb species. A beautiful glimmering silver fish, with black and red fins.

DISTRIBUTION Borneo, Malayan peninsula, Sumatra, and Thailand.

TEMPERAMENT & CARE Although a peaceful fish, it must be kept with fish of its own size in an aquarium at least 6½ ft. × 1½ ft. This is a schooling species which loves to swim against a current and needs strong filtration and large regular water changes to thrive. Will eat tender plants.

BREEDING Probably not bred by hobbyists because of its size. This species is an egg-scatterer producing several thousand eggs in a single spawning.

SCHUBERTI BARB *BARBUS SEMIFASCIOLATUS*

DESCRIPTION A strong-bodied barb with a golden body and reddish fins. Above the lateral line there are several black markings and a blotch in the caudal peduncle. The wild form has a green body with several vertical stripes, and an all-gold form has been bred. Maximum size is 3 in.

DISTRIBUTION The wild form is from southeast China.

TEMPERAMENT & CARE A robust, lively fish that holds its own in a community tank but is harmless to other fish. A hardy species which can live four or five years in captivity.

81°f
▲
70°f

BREEDING Egg-scatterer, adults will spawn every two weeks and may produce several hundred eggs at each spawning.

TIGER BARB *BARBUS TETRAZONA*

DESCRIPTION A deep-bodied barb which grows to a maximum size of nearly 3 in. The body is brownish yellow with four black vertical stripes running through the eye; just in front of, and behind, the dorsal fin; and through the caudal peduncle. Lots of different color morphs are known.

DISTRIBUTION Borneo, Indonesia, and Sumatra.

TEMPERAMENT & CARE A very lively species and possible bully. In a shoal they spend most of their time chasing each other but leave the other species alone. Very hardy, can live many years.

BREEDING Egg-scatterer laying about 200 eggs in plant thickets. Breeding takes place at first light and, once completed, the pair will eat any eggs they can find.

79°f
▲
70°f

CHERRY BARB *BARBUS TITTEYA*

DESCRIPTION A beautiful small barb (2 in.), lovely cherry red males and pinkish brown females. A dark lateral line runs through the eye to the caudal peduncle. This is strongly marked in females and immature males but fades in adult males.
DISTRIBUTION Sri Lanka.
TEMPERAMENT & CARE A very peaceful barb and good community fish. This is less of a schooling fish than many barbs and is best kept in pairs. A hardy robust species that will live many years in captivity.

81°f ▲ 70°f

BREEDING Egg-scatterer, lays eggs in plant thickets. Up to 300 eggs are produced in one spawning. The parents are avid egg eaters and will devour all they can.

CLOWN LOACH *BOTIA MACRACANTHUS*

DESCRIPTION A flat-bellied, high-backed loach with four pairs of barbels. Yellow-bodied with three black bands running vertically through it. The first passes through the eye, the second is just in front of the dorsal fin, and the third starts in the dorsal fin, passes through the body, and ends in the anal fin. The other fins are reddish orange. It develops to a maximum size of 1 ft.
DISTRIBUTION Borneo, Indonesia, and Sumatra.
TEMPERAMENT & CARE A peaceful species cohabiting well with fish of a similar size. Feels more secure if kept with

group and provided with some hiding places.
BREEDING A seasonal egg-scatterer. Breeds during the rainy season in fast-flowing waters. Rarely bred in captivity.

81°f ▲ 73°f

CHAIN BOTIA *BOTIA SIDTHIMUNKI*

DESCRIPTION A slender golden yellow fish with a black horizontal stripe from the eye to caudal peduncle and another across the back. About eight vertical bars are also found along the flanks. Maximum size just over 2 in.

DISTRIBUTION Northern India and Thailand.

TEMPERAMENT & CARE A peaceful schooling fish, ideal for community tanks. It is hardy, eats all foods, and even hunts out the scraps that fall between the pieces of gravel.

79°f
▲
72°f

BREEDING Only recently bred in captivity for the first time. It is said to be an egg-scatterer which lays its eggs into the gravel and only spawns at certain times of the year.

ZEBRA DANIO *BRACHYDANIO RERIO*

DESCRIPTION A long slender species with lovely blue horizontal stripes the full length of its body and into the fins. Males have gold between the blue and females have silver coloration. Maximum size 2 in.

DISTRIBUTION Eastern India.

TEMPERAMENT & CARE A peaceful, fast-moving, shoaling fish which is best kept in groups of six or more. They eat all foods and are very hardy. Long-finned and various color forms are known, including the leopard danio (*Brachydanio frankei*) which was thought to be a separate species for many years.

BREEDING Easy egg-scatterer which will produce up to 100 eggs per spawning.

77°f
▲
70°f

GOLDFISH *CARASSIUS AURATUS*

DESCRIPTION The wild form is a bronzy brown color with typical carp-shaped body and single tail. From this wild fish, golden mutations were selectively bred and later different fin forms. Today there are over 100 different varieties. Males develop white pimples on the leading edges of the pectoral fins and gill covers during the breeding season.

DISTRIBUTION The wild form probably originated in China but it has now been introduced to habitats the world over.

79°f
▲
48°f

TEMPERAMENT & CARE Peaceful coldwater species. Needs a large aquarium with good filtration and aeration.

BREEDING Lays its eggs in plants during the summer months. Large pairs may produce up to 1,000 eggs per spawning.

GIANT DANIO *DANIO AEQUIPINNATUS*

DESCRIPTION A torpedo-shaped species with a mottled blue and yellow body. The fins are generally clear to grayish with a dark blotch in the middle of the caudal fin. Maximum size 4 in.

DISTRIBUTION West coast of India and Sri Lanka.

TEMPERAMENT & CARE A very lively, gregarious species which likes to be part of a shoal. They prefer clean, well-oxygenated water filtered by a power filter producing water movement. They eat all foods but feed mainly from the surface.

BREEDING Easy egg-scatterer which spawns in plant thickets and produces up to 300 eggs.

81°f
▲
70°f

RED-TAILED BLACK SHARK *EPALZEORHYNCHUS BICOLOR*

81°f
▲
73°f

DESCRIPTION A very striking fish with a black body and bright red tail. The body is torpedo-shaped, and the dorsal fin stands up high like a shark's. Maximum size 6 in.

DISTRIBUTION Thailand.

TEMPERAMENT & CARE An aggressive territorial species which is often sold as a community fish but can cause mayhem by attacking anything that comes into its territory.

It likes a cave or other hiding place and will eat all foods that sink to the bottom.

BREEDING Rarely bred but said to lay its eggs in a rocky hollow.

FLYING FOX *EPALZEORHYNCHUS KALLOPTERUS*

DESCRIPTION A very long slender species with a lovely black stripe running through the eye into the caudal fin. The body is brown above the stripe and white below. The dorsal and anal fins have black blotches in them. Maximum size 6 in.

DISTRIBUTION Borneo, Indonesia, Northern India, and Sumatra.

TEMPERAMENT & CARE While basically a peaceful fish, it is territorial against other flying foxes, so should be kept singly and with access to a cave or other hideaway.

BREEDING Unknown.

81°f
▲
70°f

SUCKING LOACH *GYRINOCHEILUS AYMONIERI*

DESCRIPTION A very strange-looking creature with a flat underside and modified mouth parts. The mouth is a sucking disk with which the fish holds on to rocks, the aquarium sides, or other surfaces. A brown stripe runs through the eye to the caudal fin, above this the body is golden brown and below it silver. Maximum size nearly 10 in.

DISTRIBUTION Northern India and Thailand.

TEMPERAMENT & CARE A territorial species as an adult. Can become a problem in a community aquarium by attacking any fish that enters its territory. It is usually included as an algae eater but there are many other species which will do this job and are not aggressive.

BREEDING Unknown.

81°f
▲
70°f

ORFE *LEUCISCUS IDUS*

DESCRIPTION A long slender-bodied fish with a dull brownish body and silvery white ventral region. A beautiful golden variety (golden orfe) with reddish fins is very popular. Maximum size said to be over 3 ft. but most only reach 1½ ft. in captivity.
DISTRIBUTION Found throughout most of continental Europe.
TEMPERAMENT & CARE A peaceful coldwater species ideal for large ponds and sometimes kept in aquariums. They eat all foods but, when adults, prefer live insects and small fish.

BREEDING Spawns in late spring and early summer among plants in shallow water.

70°f
▲
39°f

CHINESE WEATHER LOACH *MISGURNUS ANGUILLICAUDATUS*

DESCRIPTION Long and slender with a down-turned mouth having barbels around it. The coloration tends to be individual with many different races in the wild. Body color is often light brown becoming white along the belly, overlaid with brown spots and mottling over the whole body. Maximum size nearly 10 in.
DISTRIBUTION China, Korea, Japan, and parts of Siberia.
TEMPERAMENT & CARE A peaceful, nocturnal bottom-dweller, stays half buried in the substrate during the day. Hides in caves or rocks. Feeds from the bottom. Must be

specially fed in a community tank after the lights have been turned off or it may waste away.

BREEDING Lays eggs in plant thickets from April to July.

77°f
▲
39°f

RED SHINER *NOTROPIS LUTRENSIS*

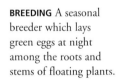

DESCRIPTION A truly beautiful coldwater fish. Males are a lovely sky-blue color with red fins. When in breeding condition, these colors are heightened and white pimples appear over the head and pectoral fins. Maximum size 3 in.

DISTRIBUTION California, Colorado, Illinois, Iowa, Minnesota, and Wyoming, as well as parts of northern Mexico.

TEMPERAMENT & CARE A shoaling coldwater species which must have clean, cool, well-oxygenated water. Can be kept in an outdoor pond

77°f
▲
59°f

during a winter that is not harsh, but displays well in an aquarium where the lovely colors can be appreciated.

BREEDING Egg-scatterer that is rarely bred in captivity. Spawns during the summer months only.

COOLIE LOACH *PANGIO KUHLII SUMATRANUS*

DESCRIPTION A very long slender snake-like species with a down-turned mouth and several pairs of barbels. The body color is pinkish gray with chocolate-brown bars across the back and down the flanks. Several different subspecies are known with different color patterns. Maximum size 4 in.

DISTRIBUTION Borneo, Java, Malaysia, Sumatra, Singapore, and Thailand.

TEMPERAMENT & CARE A secretive, nocturnal species foraging for food when the lights are out. Needs plenty of

hiding places and will even bury itself in the gravel or under subgravel filter plates. Make sure they are fed at night.

BREEDING A seasonal breeder which lays green eggs at night among the roots and stems of floating plants.

81°f
▲
72°f

HARLEQUIN *RASBORA HETEROMORPHA*

81°f
▲
70°f

DESCRIPTION A deep-bodied, almost diamond-shaped rasbora with a pinkish body color and large triangular black blotch in the rear half of the body. There are several similar species (*espei* and *hengeli*) but this one has the deepest body and largest black blotch. Maximum size almost 2 in.

DISTRIBUTION Malaysia, Singapore, Sumatra, and Thailand.

TEMPERAMENT & CARE A perfect community fish which, although quite small, can cope with larger more boisterous species. Eats all foods and lives for several years in captivity.

BREEDING Lays eggs on the underside of broad-leafed plants or in plant thickets. During spawning, the pair embrace while upside down.

SCISSORTAIL *RASBORA TRILINEATA*

DESCRIPTION A torpedo-shaped species with silvery body. Along the side from below the dorsal fin there is a black line which finishes in the caudal peduncle, and in each lobe of the caudal fin are black and yellow blotches. Maximum size 4 in.

DISTRIBUTION Borneo, Malaysia, and Sumatra.

TEMPERAMENT & CARE A very peaceful community fish which is lively and likes to be part of a shoal. Despite growing quite large, it can be kept with small fish and will live many years in captivity.

BREEDING Spawns in plant thickets where its adhesive eggs remain attached to the plants until they hatch.

81°f
▲
70°f

EXCLAMATION SPOT RASBORA *RASBORA UROPHTHALMA*

DESCRIPTION One of the miniatures of the fish world, adults grow to under 1 in. Both sexes have a dark band running down the side from behind the gill cover to in front of the caudal peduncle. Here a black spot edged in gold shines out. The male's fins have red and black markings. There is a reddish hue to the body.

DISTRIBUTION Sumatra.

TEMPERAMENT & CARE Despite its small size, it copes well in a community of small fish. Its small mouth can only take small foods such as crushed flake and newly hatched brine shrimp or sieved *Daphnia*.

BREEDING Lays eggs among dense plant growth in very soft acidic water.

81°f
▲
70°f

BITTERLING *RHODEUS SERICEUS AMERUS*

DESCRIPTION A deep-bodied species. Females have a silvery body with a bluish sheen. Males have red in the dorsal and anal fins plus a red iris to the top of the eye. Maximum size 3 in.

DISTRIBUTION Much of Europe and into western Asia.

TEMPERAMENT & CARE A fascinating, lively, coldwater fish eating all foods and fitting in well with other fish of a similar size.

BREEDING One of the most unusual members of this group. Females develop a huge ovipositor during the breeding season which deposits eggs inside a swan mussel. Here eggs and young develop until they are about four weeks old.

75°f
▲
61°f

WHITE CLOUD MOUNTAIN MINNOW *TANICHTHYS ALBONUBES*

DESCRIPTION The slender body is reddish brown paling to white on the belly. From the eye to the caudal peduncle, there is a lovely iridescent green stripe which glows when the fish are young. The fins have splashes of red and may be edged in green. Maximum size just over 1½ in.

DISTRIBUTION Southern China, particularly in the streams near the White Mountain.

TEMPERAMENT & CARE A lively schooling fish. It does well in a tropical aquarium, a coldwater tank indoors, or an outside pond during the summer months. Eats all foods and likes clean, well-oxygenated water.

BREEDING Egg-scatterer that spawns in plant thickets.

75°f
▲
63°f

Catfish
SUBORDER *Siluroidei*

Catfish can be found almost all over the world

and inhabit just about every part of the aquatic habitat. Some species

are predominantly plant-eaters, while others are predators that

will eat anything living. Only a few species live in marine habitats,

and these are said to move into brackish water to breed.

Many species care for their eggs and young,

and there are great differences between the reproductive

strategies employed.

There are thought to be over 1,000 species in the suborder,

all of which are scaleless and have a Weberian ossicle.

The Weberian ossicle is also known as the Weberian apparatus.

This was derived from the first four vertebrae which link the

inner ear to the swim bladder and help amplify sound.

BRISTLE-NOSE CATFISH *ANCISTRUS DOLICHOPTERUS*

DESCRIPTION A strange looking, sucker-mouthed catfish with large branching bristles around the mouth and on the male's head. The body color is mottled brown as are the fins. The front rays of the pectoral fins are thick, sharp spines. Maximum size nearly 5 in.

DISTRIBUTION Fast-flowing streams of the Amazon.

TEMPERAMENT & CARE A nocturnal fish rarely seen during the day and only then when it is hungry or if the water quality has deteriorated. Feed lots of vegetable matter like lettuce leaves.

81°f
▲
70°f

BREEDING The pair spawn under rocks or bog wood after which the female is chased away and the male sits on the eggs and young until they are large enough to take care of themselves.

BRONZE CORYDORAS *CORYDORAS AENEUS*

DESCRIPTION The most popular corydoras species. Large iridescent green patch on each side of body from the gill cover to the caudal peduncle. The mouth is down-turned and has several pairs of barbels. Maximum size 2½ in.

DISTRIBUTION Brazil, Colombia, Ecuador, Peru, Trinidad, and Venezuela.

TEMPERAMENT & CARE An active species, even during the day, this is a good catfish species for a community aquarium. It will never hassle other fish and rarely succumbs to disease. Tablet, frozen, and live foods should be included in their diet.

BREEDING Plasters eggs over the aquarium back and sides as well as on broad-leafed plants.

81°f
▲
70°f

BANDED CORYDORAS *CORYDORAS BARBATUS*

81°f
70°f

DESCRIPTION A long-snouted corydoras with a golden body mottled with brown. When fully mature, males have extended dorsal and pectoral fin spines. Maximum size 4 in.

DISTRIBUTION Brazil near Rio de Janeiro and São Paulo.

TEMPERAMENT & CARE A peaceful fish which does well in an aquarium with gentle species and soft acidic water conditions. They eat any food which settles on the bottom, but most need some live food in the diet to be kept in perfect health.

BREEDING Spawns in groups of two or more pairs and produces up to 100 eggs per spawning. These are laid in clumps on the aquarium sides like small bunches of grapes.

PEPPERED CORYDORAS *CORYDORAS PALEATUS*

DESCRIPTION A brown mottled species of corydoras that is one of the most popular aquarium fish. Females are decidedly plumper and males have longer and more pointed dorsal and pectoral fins. In wild strains, males have very long extensions to these fins. Maximum size nearly 3 in.
DISTRIBUTION Argentina, Brazil, and Uruguay.
TEMPERAMENT & CARE A peaceful, hardy fish which fits in well in any community tank. Eats all foods but particularly likes small worms, such as white worms.

81°f
▲
70°f

BREEDING Plasters eggs over the aquarium sides and on broad-leafed plants. Will also spawn in a clump of Java moss or a spawning mop.

WHIPTAIL CATFISH *FARLOWELLA ACUS*

DESCRIPTION A very long, slender sucker-mouth catfish, twig-like in appearance. A very long snout sticks way out in front of the mouth. The body color is light brown with a dark brown stripe running along the sides. Maximum size nearly 5 in.
DISTRIBUTION Amazon.
TEMPERAMENT & CARE A shy, retiring species which should be kept with small quiet fish in a tank that has an abundant growth of algae. Most specimens will starve to death in captivity without such an adequate supply.

BREEDING Pairs spawn on vertical surfaces. The male guards the eggs from harm. When they are ready to hatch, he helps break them out of the egg shells.

82°f
▲
73°f

SPOTTED HOPLO *HOPLOSTERNUM THORACATUM*

DESCRIPTION A mahogany brown fish with dark, almost black, blotches over the body and fins. The body shape is long, and the mouth is forward-pointing with three pairs of long whiskers. Maximum size 6 in.

DISTRIBUTION Brazil, Guyana, Martinique, Paraguay, Peru, and Trinidad.

TEMPERAMENT & CARE Most active in the evening but may take food during the day. Usually peaceful and harmless to tankmates, but during the breeding season, males become territorial and will be aggressive toward other fish.

81°f
73°f

BREEDING Builds a bubble nest under floating vegetation into which the pair lay several hundred eggs. The male then protects the eggs until the fry hatch out and swim off.

PLECOSTOMUS *HYPOSTOMUS PUNCTATUS*

DESCRIPTION This is a large (1 ft.), flat-bodied, suckermouth catfish which has a very large sail-like dorsal fin. The first rays of the pectoral fins are thick spines that can puncture a polyethylene bag with ease and will become entangled in a net. The body color is an overall mottled brown, and the fins have a net-like pattern over them.

DISTRIBUTION Brazil.

TEMPERAMENT & CARE A peaceful community fish which is rarely active during the day and prefers to hide away in caves. A vegetarian that eats all kinds of vegetable matter, including aquarium plants.

BREEDING Spawns in a tunnel dug into the river bank. The male guards the eggs.

81°f
70°f

GHOST CATFISH *KRYPTOPTERUS BICIRRHIS*

DESCRIPTION A peculiar-looking transparent fish with long slender body and a forward-pointing pair of barbels. The body sac is silvery, and all the bone structure can be seen through the sides of the fish. Maximum size 5 in.

DISTRIBUTION Borneo, India, Indonesia, Malaysia, Sumatra, and Thailand.

TEMPERAMENT & CARE Peaceful shoaling fish which likes a strong water current. Can be sensitive to poor water quality and needs a varied diet, including some live foods.

BREEDING Egg-scatterer which lays its eggs in plant thickets. Rarely bred in the aquarium.

82°f
▲
73°f

BLUE-EYED PLECOSTOMUS *PANAQUE SUTTONI*

DESCRIPTION The black body and fins contrast strongly with the brilliant blue eye of this sucker-mouth catfish. The caudal fin is sickle-shaped, and the dorsal is large and held almost vertically. Maximum size 7 in.

DISTRIBUTION Colombia and Guyana.

TEMPERAMENT & CARE A quiet, shy fish which needs plenty of caves to hide in, and clean, well-filtered water. Must have aeration to raise the oxygen content and be fed with plenty of vegetable matter. Loves cucumber and peas.

BREEDING Unknown.

81°f
▲
73°f

POLKA-DOT CATFISH *SYNODONTIS ANGELICUS*

81°f
▲
73°f

DESCRIPTION The velvety black body contrasts sharply with the white polka dots which cover the body. The fins are banded black and white and the first ray of the pectoral fin is a sharp spine. Maximum size 7 in.
DISTRIBUTION Cameroon and Zaire.

TEMPERAMENT & CARE Peaceful schooling, nocturnal species which likes to hide in caves during the day. At night it digs in the substrate searching for food and will uproot plants. Needs some live foods in its diet to thrive.
BREEDING Unknown but possibly seasonal pit-spawner.

Characins

SUBORDER *Characoidei*

There are a huge number of characin species in the world,

many of which are yet to be described by science. At the moment,

there are about 1,000 species known from South America and at least

200 from the African continent, but more are being discovered all the

time. The fact that they are found on both continents helps prove

that Africa and South America were joined at one stage and that

the characoidei had already evolved at this time. Since the continental

split is thought to have occurred in Mesozoic times when Dinosaurs

still lived, this means characins were swimming around in the rivers

with these fantastic reptiles.

MARBLED HEADSTANDER *ABRAMITES HYPSELONOTUS*

DESCRIPTION A deep-bodied fish with a marbled brown and fawn body. This species has a habit of swimming with its head down and resting almost vertically with the tail uppermost. Maximum size nearly 5 in.

DISTRIBUTION Found throughout the Amazon and Orinoco river systems.

TEMPERAMENT & CARE A loner which can be kept in a mixed community tank of similar-sized fish but not with its own species. Likes plenty of cover in the form of bog wood and plants but will eat new shoots.

BREEDING Unknown in captivity.

81°f
▲
73°f

STRIPED ANOSTOMUS *ANOSTOMUS ANOSTOMUS*

DESCRIPTION A slender-bodied fish with yellow and black stripes running the full body length. There is a splash of blood red at the base of the dorsal and caudal fins. Maximum size 6 in.

DISTRIBUTION Colombia, Guyana, and Venezuela.

TEMPERAMENT & CARE Best kept in a large school of six or more fish or as individual specimens in a community aquarium. Will eat all foods but will nibble plants when nothing else is available.

BREEDING Lays adhesive eggs in plant thickets near the surface.

81°f
▲
73°f

BLOODFIN *APHOCHARAX ANISITSI*

DESCRIPTION A lovely silvery fish with blood red in the pelvic, anal, and caudal fins. It used to be very common in the hobby but is rarely imported today. It can live up to 10 years in captivity and grows to 2 in. in body length.
DISTRIBUTION Argentina.
TEMPERAMENT & CARE Peaceful schooling fish which is constantly on the move. Eats anything and is very hardy. Likes plenty of swimming room, but some plant thickets should also be included in the aquarium setup.

81°f
▲
72°f

BREEDING Easy egg-scatterer that lays its eggs in plant thickets near the surface.

BLIND CAVE TETRA *ASTYANAX FASCIATUS MEXICANUS*

DESCRIPTION This is the cave form of *Astynax fasciatus mexicanus*. As with most cave fish, the eyes are reduced to almost nothing and all pigmentation has been lost. The result is a pinkish fish with clear fins and no visible eyes. Maximum size 3 in.
DISTRIBUTION Found in underground rivers flowing through Mexican cave systems.
TEMPERAMENT & CARE Peaceful fish which, despite having no eyes, can find food as quickly as other fish. Can be kept in most community tanks and will eat all foods.

BREEDING Scatters eggs in open water. Spawning usually follows a water change.

79°f
▲
68°f

MARBLED HATCHETFISH *Carnegiella strigata strigata*

DESCRIPTION The body is very deep and resembles the head of an ax. They have very large pectoral fins that look a lot like wings and perform the same function, enabling this fish to skim across the water surface when frightened. The body color is marbled black, silver, and brown, and the fish grows to only just over 1½ in.

DISTRIBUTION Peru.

TEMPERAMENT & CARE Peaceful, although skittish fish which should be kept in a shoal of six or more. Will eat all floating foods and loves wingless fruit flies and other insects that float on the surface.

BREEDING Scatters semiadhesive eggs among floating plant roots.

BLACK WIDOW TETRA *Gymnocorymbus ternetzi*

DESCRIPTION A deep-bodied tetra with black dorsal and anal fins and a silvery body with several vertical black markings. The anal fin is very large and has many rays in it. Maximum size 2 in.

DISTRIBUTION Bolivia.

TEMPERAMENT & CARE Peaceful shoaling fish which is ideal for the community tank. Likes some plant cover and tends to hide among this as it gets older. Eats all foods but likes some live food in the diet.

BREEDING Prolific fish which scatters its eggs in plant thickets.

BLACK NEON TETRA *HYPHESSOBRYCON HERBERTAXELRODI*

DESCRIPTION Typical tetra with a glowing green line from behind the eye to the caudal peduncle. Below this the body is black, becoming silvery on the belly. The upper iris is red, and the fish grows to a maximum size of only just over 1½ in.
DISTRIBUTION Mato Grosso, Brazil.
TEMPERAMENT & CARE Peaceful community fish which will form schools with other fish. Likes insects and other meaty foods in its diet and will eat newborn livebearers.

81°f
▲
72°f

BREEDING Needs very soft and acidic water to breed in. Thrives on lots of live foods. Spawns in plant thickets.

EMPEROR TETRA *NEMATOBRYCON PALMERI*

DESCRIPTION A beautiful fish with iridescent blue sheen to the body and trident-shaped tail. Below the lateral line, the body is black, becoming white on the belly. The iris of the eye is blue in males and green in females. Maximum size just over 2 in.
DISTRIBUTION Colombia.
TEMPERAMENT & CARE Peaceful fish which tends to swim around plant thickets in groups of three or four. Males will occasionally spar, but no real damage is done during these encounters.

BREEDING Spawns in plants near the surface, but the semiadhesive eggs often fall into the substrate and continue their development there.

81°f
▲
70°f

NEON TETRA *PARACHEIRODON INNESI*

82°f
▲
72°f

DESCRIPTION A neon blue line runs from the eye to just before the origin of the adipose fin. The lower half of the body is silver in front and blood red toward the rear. This is one of the best known aquarium fish, and it grows to only just over 1½ in.

DISTRIBUTION Peru.

TEMPERAMENT & CARE Peaceful community fish which, despite its small size, can hold its own with larger fish. Likes to have some planted areas to retire to. Hardy and will live several years in captivity.

BREEDING Spawns in open water after which the eggs sink into the substrate and hatch the next day. Must have very soft acidic water for the eggs to hatch.

CONGO TETRA *PHENACOGRAMMUS INTERRUPTUS*

DESCRIPTION A beautiful
characin with a rainbow of
colors on the body. Males
develop extensions to the
dorsal, anal, and the center of
the caudal fin. Full grown
males reach nearly 3 in. and
females nearly 2½ in.
DISTRIBUTION Zaire.
TEMPERAMENT & CARE Peaceful
although somewhat timid
schooling fish which likes lots
of open swimming space
combined with some areas of
dense plant growth. Eats all
foods from the top and
midwater area of the tank and
will nibble plant shoots.

BREEDING Scatters nonadhesive
eggs in shallow open water.
Most spawnings occur at first
light.

RED-BELLIED PIRANHA *SERRASALMUS NATTERERI*

DESCRIPTION A deep-bodied
fish with a black-spotted silver
body when young. At this age
there is a red patch behind the
gill cover, and the anal fin is
red. As an adult the body is an
overall brownish silver and the
throat and ventral region are
blood red. Maximum size
11 in.
DISTRIBUTION Widely
distributed throughout the
Amazon and Orinoco rivers.
TEMPERAMENT & CARE A nasty,
vicious predator which will
bite anything which threatens
it. While it likes to feed on
live fish, most specimens will
learn to take dead foods, like
pieces of fish or meat.

BREEDING Pit-spawner in
which the pair initially guard
the nest but eventually the
male chases his mate away.

Once the fry are free-
swimming, he should
be removed.

Cichlids
Suborder Percoidei, Family Cichlidae

Cichlids are a very large family of freshwater fish

distributed throughout Africa, Central and South America, India,

and parts of the Middle East. Various estimates exist of the

number of species contained in the family, and there are in excess of

900 described species throughout the world. Most protect their

eggs in some way, and many make interesting aquarium fish.

Few species are good community fish.

In recent times, several species of tilapia have been

introduced all over the world as useful food fish. These, unfortunately,

have caused the rapid decline of native species.

PANDA DWARF CICHLID *APISTOGRAMMA NIJSSENI*

DESCRIPTION Males are bluish with a yellow belly and orange-edged caudal fin. Females are yellow with greenish black blotches and look like a completely different species. Maximum size for males is nearly 2½ in. and for females just over 1½ in.
DISTRIBUTION Peru.
TEMPERAMENT & CARE A somewhat timid territorial species that can only be combined with quiet, peaceful fish. Likes lots of plants in the tank and areas where each male may define his own territory. Include some caves made out of rocks.

BREEDING Cave-spawner. The female looks after the eggs, the male guards the territory.

81°f
73°f

OSCAR *ASTRONOTUS OCELLATUS*

DESCRIPTION This large (1 ft.) cichlid has matt scales. They are mottled dark and light brown to gray with splashes of orange, particularly in the fins. A "peacock's eye" adorns the caudal peduncle and is edged in bright orange. Several color forms exist.
DISTRIBUTION Amazon Basin.
TEMPERAMENT & CARE While not really aggressive, this fish forms a nuclear family which guards its own territory and can only be housed in a large aquarium. This must have a deep substrate and some rockwork.

BREEDING Open-spawners which lay their eggs on a rock. The adult pair look after their young until they are able to take care of themselves. Spawns of 2,000 are known.

72°f
82°f

STRIPED PIKE CICHLID *CRENICICHLA STRIGATA*

DESCRIPTION A large (16 in.) slender-bodied fish with horizontal stripes running the full length of the body when young. These stripes fade as they mature, and females develop a red stomach.
DISTRIBUTION Brazil & Guyana.
TEMPERAMENT & CARE A large predator which can only be kept by itself or with others of its own species if they are reared together. Needs a very large aquarium with lots of roots and rockwork to provide hiding places.

BREEDING Cave-spawner in which both parents care for the eggs and young.

JEWEL CICHLID *HEMICHROMIS BIMACULATUS*

DESCRIPTION A chunky-bodied, medium-sized cichlid reaching a maximum size of 6 in. As a juvenile, the body is a dull olive green with three black spots on the sides. In breeding condition, they turn a beautiful blood red with blue spots.
DISTRIBUTION Coastal Africa from Guinea to Liberia.
TEMPERAMENT & CARE Aggressive territorial species that can only be kept as a breeding pair or group of youngsters. Likes a deep substrate to dig in and plenty of caves and rocks. Plants are often dug up.

BREEDING Eggs are laid in caves, and both parents nurture them. Later the fry are moved to pits dug in the substrate.

REGAN'S JULIE *JULIDOCHROMIS REGANI*

DESCRIPTION A slender-bodied cichlid which grows to a maximum size of nearly 4 in, although males are usually smaller. They have a lovely yellow and black horizontally striped body.
DISTRIBUTION Lake Tanganyika.
TEMPERAMENT & CARE A territorial species which is best kept as a breeding pair and their offspring. Include lots of caves and rockwork and some hardy well-rooted plants for cover.

81°f
▲
75°f

BREEDING Spawns in caves. The pair move free-swimming fry into a pit dug in the substrate.

LYRETAIL CICHLID *NEOLAMPROLOGUS BRICHARDI*

DESCRIPTION A very pretty cichlid with a distinctive lyre-shaped tail. The body is gray with a dark line through the eye and a black spot on the operculum. Just in front of this spot is a golden blotch. Maximum size 4 in.
DISTRIBUTION Tanganyika.
TEMPERAMENT & CARE Likes to form schools of its own species and will tolerate other similar-sized peaceful fish. Must have very hard alkaline water and needs to be fed plenty of live foods.

BREEDING Spawns in caves after which the female guards the eggs. Later broods are cared for by their older siblings as well as their parents.

81°f
▲
72°f

AURATUS MBUNA *MELANOCHROMIS AURATUS*

DESCRIPTION A beautiful slender-bodied cichlid with very differently colored sexes. Females are golden yellow with two black horizontal stripes and several white ones. Mature males are black with two white horizontal stripes. Maximum size 4 in.

DISTRIBUTION Lake Malawi.

TEMPERAMENT & CARE An aggressive territorial species which must be kept in a Malawi cichlid tank with lots of rockwork and hiding places. Can be kept as a breeding group on their own, in which case combine one male with at least four females.

79°f

72°f

BREEDING Males mate with any ripe female who then picks up the eggs and broods them in her mouth. She also cares for the fry for a week after they initially leave her mouth.

RAM *PAPILIOCHROMIS RAMIREZI*

DESCRIPTION A beautiful small (nearly 2½ in.) cichlid with an overall blue body color and yellow to red stomach. A large black spot adorns the middle of the body, and a vertical black stripe runs through the eye. The fins are reddish with electric blue spangles, and the front rays of the dorsal are black.

DISTRIBUTION Colombia and Venezuela.

TEMPERAMENT & CARE A peaceful community fish which loves lots of plant growth and places to hide, but will spend most of the time out and about once it has settled in. Usually lives only three years.

BREEDING Open-spawner with both parents protecting the eggs and young. Once the babies are free-swimming, the parents move them into a breeding pit.

82°f

73°f

KRIBENSIS *PELVICACHROMIS PULCHER*

81°f
▲
70°f

DESCRIPTION One of the most underrated small (3 in.) cichlids available. As young fish they are a dull olive color with a dark stripe running from the eye to the caudal peduncle. Once mature, however, they develop a beautiful red stomach and females have lime green patches before and after the red area.

DISTRIBUTION Nigeria.

TEMPERAMENT & CARE A peaceful territorial species which will live happily in a community tank that contains rocky hiding places. Likes a well-planted tank and will dig in the substrate but rarely uproot plants.

BREEDING Cave-spawners, the female looks after eggs and young while the male guards the territory.

ZEBRA MBUNA *PSEUDOTROPHEUS ZEBRA*

DESCRIPTION A typical Mbuna species which has a huge range of different color forms. The typical color is blue with lots of vertical black bars on the body and a few false egg spots on the anal fin. Some color forms are gold with black blotches, and others have no black markings. Maximum size nearly 5 in.

DISTRIBUTION Lake Malawi.

TEMPERAMENT & CARE An aggressive species suitable for its own species tank or a mixed Malawi tank. Needs lots of rocks and hiding places. Keep one male to three females.

BREEDING Male mates with any ripe female. The eggs are mouthbrooded by the female who tends the fry for a week after she has released them.

ANGELFISH *PTEROPHYLLUM SCALARE*

DESCRIPTION A deep-bodied fish with extended dorsal, anal, and pelvic fins. The caudal fin also has filaments from its top and bottom lobe. Many different color patterns have been developed, but the wild form is silver with four vertical stripes. Maximum size 4 in.

DISTRIBUTION Amazon basin.

TEMPERAMENT & CARE As young fish they form a school and spend much of their time together. Once mature they form pairs which have their own territory. Basically peaceful but will eat any very small fish and, when large, may bully tankmates.

BREEDING Open-spawners which lay their eggs on a plant leaf or other suitable vertical surface. The pair look after their eggs and the young.

GREEN DISCUS *SYMPHYSODON AEQUIFASCIATUS*

86°f
▲
79°f

DESCRIPTION A discus-shaped fish bred in a variety of color forms. The wild form has a brownish body with faint vertical bars. The iris is red. Throughout the fins and over much of the head, there is a green pattern. Maximum size 6 in.

DISTRIBUTION Amazon.

TEMPERAMENT & CARE Considered difficult and should be kept in a tank on its own. Needs a deep, well-planted aquarium and soft acidic water. The diet should contain lots of live food.

BREEDING Open-spawner which lays its eggs on any suitable vertical surface. The pair look after the eggs and fry, which feed on secretions from the parents' bodies.

Gobies and related fish

SUBORDER Gobioidei

This is a very large group of fish which have two

dorsal fins and are commonly found in brackish and marine habitats.

Some species have adapted to freshwater and are kept by aquarists.

Most have their pelvic fins fused into a single fin that is used as a

sucking disk, and many have a reduced swim bladder so that they

scuttle about the bottom. One of the biggest problems with this group

is that they rarely take commercial foods and need to be fed live or

frozen foods if they are to survive in captivity.

BUMBLEBEE GOBY *BRACHYGOBIUS XANTHOZONA*

DESCRIPTION A pretty little (just over 1½ in.)
fish with a yellow body with four vertical black
bars. It has a reduced swim bladder so spends
most of its time on the bottom, but the pelvic
fins form a sucking disk with which it can hang
on to the tank sides if it wishes.
DISTRIBUTION Thailand and Vietnam.
TEMPERAMENT & CARE A gentle, timid species
that can only be combined with other small
peaceful fish. A territorial species which chases
other species off. Add 1 tablespoon of sea salt
to each 2 gallons of water and feed only live
foods.
BREEDING Cave-spawner with the male
guarding the eggs and fry.

81°f
▲
72°f

PEACOCK GOBY *TATEURNDINA OCELLICAUDA*

DESCRIPTION Beautiful blue
goby with red and yellow
markings in the body and fins.
In the caudal peduncle is a
black spot, and the ventral
region of the body is yellow.
This fish has a normal swim
bladder. Maximum size 2 in.
DISTRIBUTION New Guinea.
TEMPERAMENT & CARE Peaceful
hardy fish which fits in well in
a small fish community. Likes
plenty of plant growth, rocks,
or other objects to hide in and
around. Rarely accepts
commercial foods and should
therefore be fed live foods to
be at their best.

BREEDING Cave-spawner with
the male looking after the
eggs.

81°f
▲
72°f

Gouramis and other labyrinth fish

SUBORDER *Anabantoidei*

Gouramis and other labyrinth fish have developed

an organ called the labyrinth that enables them to take gulps of

atmospheric air and extract oxygen from it. This means they can

survive in very badly polluted water when other fish would die.

Two main methods of reproduction are used in the group:

mouthbrooding and bubble nesting. In the latter, the males build

a nest of bubbles coated in saliva into which the eggs are placed.

In mouthbrooders, the eggs are taken into the male's mouth and held

until the fry are free-swimming.

SIAMESE FIGHTING FISH *BETTA SPLENDENS*

82°f
▲
70°f

DESCRIPTION An incredibly beautiful fish. The males have extended fins of red, blue, black, white, green, or any combination of these colors. In females the colors tend to be muted, and the fins are short. A twin-tailed form is known. Maximum size nearly 2½ in.
DISTRIBUTION Cambodia and Thailand.

TEMPERAMENT & CARE While the males will attack and kill each other, several females can usually be housed in one tank. In a normal community tank with fast-moving fish, the males are often subjected to bullying. Use plant cover to reduce this problem.
BREEDING Builds a bubble nest. If the female is not ready to spawn, she will be damaged or killed.

DWARF GOURAMI *COLISA LALIA*

DESCRIPTION A deep-bodied, small (2 in.) fish which is truly beautiful. Females are silvery with blue vertical bands and males are rusty red with the same blue bands. The male throat is also blue, and the fins are mottled red and blue. There are several color forms.
DISTRIBUTION India and possibly Borneo.
TEMPERAMENT & CARE Peaceful community fish which likes plenty of plant cover to hide in. Once settled they become very tame and will even feed out of your fingers.

82°f
▲
70°f

BREEDING Builds a bubble nest including plant material. Male guards the eggs and fry until they are free-swimming.

ORNATE CTENOPOMA *CTENOPOMA ANSORGII*

DESCRIPTION A slender-bodied species with lovely yellow to orange colored body and vertical black stripes. Some fish have a turquoise green body color. This may depend on diet or more likely where it was collected. Maximum size 3 in.
DISTRIBUTION Congo and Zaire.
TEMPERAMENT & CARE Not an aggressive fish but will eat anything it can fit into its mouth. Likes a well-planted aquarium with swimming room at the front. Feed only live and frozen foods.

BREEDING Rarely bred bubble-nester.

82°f
▲
75°f

KISSING GOURAMI *HELOSTOMA TEMMINCKII*

DESCRIPTION A large (1 ft.) gourami which has a compressed body and large forward-pointing lips. The body color is either green or pink depending on the color form, and there is a pearly sheen to it which is very attractive.

DISTRIBUTION Java and Thailand.

TEMPERAMENT & CARE Peaceful species which can be mixed with similar-sized fish. Likes a large aquarium with lots of algae growth on which to browse. Eats all vegetable matter but will also take flake and live foods.

BREEDING Spawns under plants at the surface. The eggs float to the surface where the parents ignore them.

PARADISE FISH *MACROPODUS OPERCULARIS*

DESCRIPTION Both sexes are a rusty red with vertical blue bands along the whole body. The gill cover is red with an iridescent blue spot toward the outer edge. Males have longer fins and are brighter colored. Maximum size 4 in.

DISTRIBUTION China, Korea, Malacca, Taiwan, and the Ryukyu Islands.

TEMPERAMENT & CARE Peaceful with other fish, but adult males fight and will kill each other. Although considered a tropical fish, they will live happily at temperatures as low as 59°F.

BREEDING Builds a bubble nest underneath vegetation. After spawning, the male cares for the eggs and young until they are free-swimming.

GIANT GOURAMI *OSPHRONEMUS GOURAMI*

DESCRIPTION One of the monsters of the aquarium world, growing up to 2 ft. in body length. When young, the body is brown with darker vertical bands, but as they grow the color fades to a grayish brown without the bands and the lips become very thick and rubbery.
DISTRIBUTION China, India, Java, Malaysia.
TEMPERAMENT & CARE Peaceful enough, but size prohibits inclusion in all but the largest community tank. Likes a lot of vegetable matter in the diet and can be trained to take food from your fingers.

A great fish if you have a large tank.
BREEDING Bubble-nest builder.

82°f
▲
70°f

THREE SPOT, BLUE, CROSBY, OR GOLD GOURAMI
TRICHOGASTER TRICHOPTERUS

DESCRIPTION There are many different color forms of this fish, ranging from three spotted forms with a blue body to golden fish with a red eye. All have a very large anal fin and their pelvic fins developed into two long "feelers." Maximum size nearly 5 in.
DISTRIBUTION Burma, Malaysia, Sumatra, Thailand, and Vietnam.
TEMPERAMENT & CARE Peaceful with similar-sized fish. Eats all foods and is very hardy. It can tolerate poor water quality and diet better than most other fish.

BREEDING Builds a bubble nest.

82°f
▲
70°f

Halfbeaks

SUBORDER *Exocoetoidei*

The halfbeaks belong to a group of fish

that come mainly from marine habitats and include the flying fish.

They have an elongated lower jaw, and the dorsal and anal fins

are positioned towards the rear of the body. They are predators

which feed from the water's surface and have the reputation of being

difficult to maintain in captivity. While some species live in

brackish water, many do not and will suffer if they are kept

in such conditions. Most members of the suborder are egg-layers,

but many species of halfbeak are livebearers or at least

internally fertilize their eggs.

WRESTLING HALFBEAK *DERMOGENYS PUSILLUS*

DESCRIPTION A slender-bodied fish with long lower jaw. The dorsal and anal fins are set well back on the body, and part of the anal fin is modified into a copulatory organ. Maximum size 2 in.

DISTRIBUTION Indonesia, Malaysia, Singapore, and Thailand.

TEMPERAMENT & CARE A peaceful, timid fish which becomes frightened in a community aquarium. Best kept in a species tank with lots of floating plants and hard, alkaline water. Add 1 teaspoon of sea salt per gallon of water. Feeds on live foods at the surface, like fruit flies or mosquito larvae. Can be trained to take carnivore flake food.

BREEDING Livebearer which produces fry after a gestation period of about six weeks. Maximum brood size 30.

81°f
▲
73°f

CELEBES HALFBEAK *NOMORHAMPHUS CELEBENSIS*

DESCRIPTION A slender-bodied fish with a shorter lower jaw than many halfbeaks. The body is yellowish, and the fins have red and black on them. The lower jaw of many males is thickened, black, and turned down. This occurs when the beak has been broken. Maximum size nearly 3 in.

DISTRIBUTION Celebes island, Indonesia.

TEMPERAMENT & CARE A robust species that can live in a community aquarium providing its tankmates are too large to eat. It likes cool, well-oxygenated fresh water. This is a predator which needs lots of live foods in the diet and, despite the mouth shape, will feed off the bottom.

BREEDING Livebearer producing monthly broods of up to 15.

75°f
▲
70°f

Perches

SUBORDER *Percoidei*

The perches include two groups already

mentioned in this book, the cichlids and labyrinths.

These have been separated from the rest of the suborder

because aquarists look upon them as distinct groups in their

own right. Many of the species in this group have two dorsal fins and

come from brackish or marine habitats. They include the North

American sunfish, which are superb game fish, and some very strange

species with unusual feeding adaptations. On the whole, they are not

kept as aquarium fish, but a couple of important species are

regularly found, so these have been included here.

GLASS FISH *CHANDA RANGA*

81°f
70°f

DESCRIPTION A transparent fish with two dorsal fins and silvery body sac. Apart from a hint of brown in the fins and an electric blue edging to the second dorsal and the anal fin, this is a colorless fish. They are, however, being injected with fluorescent dyes to create garish creatures. No reputable dealer will sell this kind of mutilated fish. Maximum size nearly 3 in.

DISTRIBUTION Bengal, Burma, and India.
TEMPERAMENT & CARE A timid schooling fish that likes some plant cover in the tank. Only keep it with slow-moving fish which will not frighten it. Must be fed some live foods.
BREEDING Lays eggs among plants.

ARCHER FISH *TOXOTES JACULATRIX*

82°f
▲
77°f

DESCRIPTION A robust-bodied fish with a large up-turned mouth, and dorsal and anal fins positioned toward the rear. The body color is silvery with about five blotches along the sides. Maximum size 8 in.
DISTRIBUTION Australia, India, and southeastern Asia.

TEMPERAMENT & CARE Likes to be kept in a group, but larger fish will bully small ones. Feeds on insects that fall on the water's surface, but if none are forthcoming, they will shoot their own down with jets of water or jump out of the water to catch them. Add 1½ teaspoons of sea salt per gallon of water.
BREEDING Unknown.

Toothcarps – Egglaying

SUBORDER Cyprinodontoidei, Family Cyprinodontidae

This is a large family of small fresh and brackish-water

fish which are found in most tropical freshwater rivers of the world.

They can even be found in subtropical and cool

temperate regions as well. All have teeth in their jaws but are

generally peaceful fish which will fit in well in a community tank.

Most are straight-forward egg layers which hang their eggs

among plant leaves, but some bury their eggs in mud, and

others carry them around with them for several hours or even weeks

until they hatch. Many species have incredible colors

and make excellent aquarium fish.

LYRETAIL KILLIFISH *APHYOSEMION AUSTRALE*

75°f

70°f

DESCRIPTION A very slender-bodied species with incredibly beautiful coloration. The wild form has a greenish body with red spots and red, yellow, and white fins. Several color forms are known, including gold and chocolate. All the fins are extended but particularly the top and bottom lobes of the tail. Maximum size 2 in.
DISTRIBUTION Africa.

TEMPERAMENT & CARE Peaceful, shy species which likes plenty of plant cover in the aquarium. Males may become pugnacious when breeding, and it is best to keep two or three females to every male.
BREEDING Use soft acidic water for breeding. Hangs eggs among plant leaves close to the substrate, and they take two weeks to hatch.

JAMAICAN KILLIFISH *CUBANICHTHYS PENGELLEYI*

DESCRIPTION Males are high-backed and deep-bodied fish with large black-edged scales. The body color is golden to bluish with a dark horizontal stripe through the eye to the caudal peduncle. Females are more slender, have smaller fins and lack the blue and gold. Maximum size 2 in.
DISTRIBUTION Jamaica.
TEMPERAMENT & CARE A moderately peaceful fish that can be kept in a community aquarium, providing some plant cover is included. Males are aggressive toward one another; the weaker fish are often bullied to death.

BREEDING Lays a few eggs each day in plants near the substrate. The eggs have a two-week incubation.

77°f
▲
73°f

BLACK-FINNED PEARL FISH *CYNOLEBIAS NIGRIPINNIS*

DESCRIPTION A stocky-bodied fish with mottled brown females and iridescent bluish-white spotted black males. This is an annual species which grows very quickly to its adult size of just over 1½ in. It will live only a year or so.
DISTRIBUTION Argentina.
TEMPERAMENT & CARE A lively species that can be kept in a community aquarium. Males often squabble and nip each other's fins. Feed live and frozen foods. Keep in moderately hard water with a neutral pH.

73°f
▲
70°f

BREEDING Buries eggs in a peat substrate. The substrate is then removed and kept moist for three months before being put back in water for the eggs to hatch.

AMERICAN FLAGFISH *JORDANELLA FLORIDAE*

75°f
68°f

DESCRIPTION Females are olive with a large black blotch below the origin of the dorsal fin. Males have each scale edged in rusty red and the same blotch as the female. Their dorsal and anal fins are larger and mottled red. Maximum size 2 in.

DISTRIBUTION Coastal regions of North America from Florida southward to the Yucatan peninsula of Mexico.

TEMPERAMENT & CARE Males are aggressive toward one another but otherwise peaceful. Likes some plant cover and will eat all foods.

BREEDING The pair spawn at the base of plant thickets after which the female should be removed. The male guards the eggs and young until they are free-swimming.

RACHOW'S NOTHO *NOTHOBRANCHIUS RACHOVII*

DESCRIPTION Males are truly stunning with a red basic body color overlaid with iridescent blue. The dorsal and anal fins are mottled blue and red. The caudal fin has a band of red, a band of orange, and a thick black edge. Females are a dull gray. Maximum size 2 in.

DISTRIBUTION Africa.

TEMPERAMENT & CARE A peaceful fish, but males are territorial. Can be kept with nonaggressive species. A species tank with a peat substrate is best. Diet should contain lots of live foods.

73°f
▲
70°f

BREEDING Substrate-spawner which needs its eggs kept in moist peat for three months before being placed in water to hatch.

GREEN LAMPEYE *PROCATOPUS ABERRANS*

DESCRIPTION The male has a beautiful blue sheen to his body. The fins are enlarged and blue with red spots. The female tends to be very plain with a silvery gray body and smaller fins. Maximum size 2 in.

DISTRIBUTION Cameroon and Nigeria.

TEMPERAMENT & CARE A peaceful schooling fish that can be kept in any small fish-community aquarium. It likes some plant cover but needs open water areas to swim in as well. Eats all foods.

BREEDING Lays its eggs down cracks in wood or stones but will also place them among the roots of floating plants. They take two weeks to hatch.

79°f
▲
70°f

Toothcarps – Livebearing

SUBORDER Cyprinodontoidei, Families Anablepidae,
Goodeidae, & Poeciliidae

This group of fish includes some of the most popular

of all aquarium fish. Most species have the male's anal fin modified

into a copulatory organ so that sperm can be channeled into the

female's vent. Once she has been fertilized, the young take from four

to eight weeks to develop and can be quite large when they are born.

Depending on the species, some females nourish their

young while they are developing. This can be done in a very

rudimentary way with the baby being born the same size as the egg

started out, or it can involve complicated feeding structures

which enable the embryo to grow significantly

during its development.

FOUR-EYED LIVEBEARER *ANABLEPS ANABLEPS*

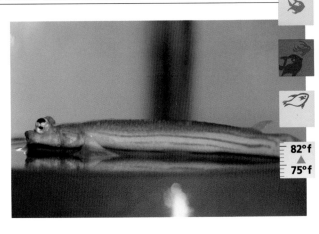

DESCRIPTION A very odd-looking creature with its eyes divided horizontally so it can see above and below the surface. The body is silvery with a series of longitudinal stripes. Males have a modified anal fin. Maximum size nearly 10 in.
DISTRIBUTION Central America and northern South America.
TEMPERAMENT & CARE A skittish, schooling fish which likes to climb out of the water onto a mud bank to sunbathe. Eats all foods but loves earthworms and other large live foods. Add 1 teaspoonful of sea salt per gallon of water.

82°f
▲
75°f

BREEDING Livebearer producing up to 15 fry after a six-week gestation period. These are 1¼-2 in. at birth.

PIKE LIVEBEARER *BELONESOX BELIZANUS*

DESCRIPTION A slender fish with large mouth and rows of needle-like teeth. During the day, it is dull brown across the back with a darker midlateral band and a white belly. At night, it turns almost jet black. Maximum size for males nearly 5 in. and females 11 in.
DISTRIBUTION Along the Atlantic coast from Mexico to Honduras.
TEMPERAMENT & CARE A predator that can only be kept with fish which are the same size or larger. Best kept as a pair with a shoal of feeder fish.

BREEDING Females produce broods of up to 250 every month. If the male dies, the female will continue to produce several more broods from stored sperm.

81°f
▲
70°f

RED RAINBOW GOODEID *CHARACODON LATERALIS*

DESCRIPTION Females are green with a row of black spots on the sides of some fish. Males have red fins (the anal with a notch in it) and ventral area with some black spots along the sides and black edging to the fins. Maximum size 2 in.
DISTRIBUTION Springs around the city of Durango, Mexico.
TEMPERAMENT & CARE A peaceful fish which will adapt to a community tank without problems. For breeding it is best kept in a species tank with good plant cover. Feed lots of live food.

73°f
▲
68°f

BREEDING Females produce up to 20 fry every six weeks.

EASTERN MOSQUITO FISH *GAMBUSIA HOLBROOKI*

DESCRIPTION A slender livebearer which has a gray body with a vertical band through the eyes and black speckled fins. Males possess a rod-like anal fin and reach a maximum size of just over 1 in. Females reach 2 in. A black speckled form of this species is known.
DISTRIBUTION Southeastern USA from Florida to the Rio Panuco basin in Mexico. Introduced all over the tropical world for mosquito control.
TEMPERAMENT & CARE A fin-nipper which cannot be kept with other species. Needs a species tank with some plant cover. Feed lots of live foods.

BREEDING Females produce up to 60 fry every four to eight weeks.

86°f
▲
59°f

ONE-SIDED LIVEBEARER *JENYNSIA LINEATA*

DESCRIPTION A slender green fish with black lines and spots along the sides. Males have an anal fin which has been modified into a copulatory organ bent to the left or right. Females have their vent covered on one side. Maximum size, males just over 1½ in., females nearly 3 in.

DISTRIBUTION Argentina and Brazil.

TEMPERAMENT & CARE A peaceful, timid fish which does not thrive in a community aquarium. Prefers a well-planted tank with its own kind. Must have lots of live food in the diet and hard alkaline water.

BREEDING After six to eight weeks gestation, the female will produce broods of up to 25 about half an inch long.

HUMPBACK LIMIA *LIMIA NIGROFASCIATA*

DESCRIPTION Both sexes have black vertical bars along the flanks and an overall brownish body fading to white on the stomach. As males mature, they develop a high back and a keel-like edge to the lower body behind the anal fin. Maximum size 2 in.

DISTRIBUTION Lake Miragoane, Haiti.

TEMPERAMENT & CARE Peaceful community fish which fits in well with most other fish of a similar size. Live foods are important to their health, and they should be fed several times a week.

BREEDING Females produce broods of up to 40 every four weeks.

ATLANTIC MOLLY *Poecilia mexicana*

DESCRIPTION A slender molly
with bluish sides and several
darker vertical bands along the
sides with pale orange in the
fins. There is a lot of variation
in wild stocks, and this species
has been hybridized with other
mollies to produce many
different color forms.
Maximum size 4 in.
DISTRIBUTION Central America.
TEMPERAMENT & CARE Good
community fish that will fit in
with most other fish providing
they are not too timid. Needs
neutral to alkaline water
conditions and likes plenty of
growing plants in the

aquarium. For good growth
and healthy offspring, feed lots
of live foods. Must have clean,
well-filtered water.

BREEDING Females produce up
to 100 fry every month.

GUPPY *Poecilia reticulata*

DESCRIPTION The wild-form
males are very small fish with
a few spots of red, blue, green,
or black. From this
nondescript fish, hundreds of
color forms and fin shapes
have been bred. Wild females
are gray, but cultivated ones
can have larger colored fins as
well. Maximum size, males
just over 1 in., females 2 in.
DISTRIBUTION Originally
Venezuela, Trinidad, and other
islands in the area, but now
widely distributed throughout
the world for mosquito
control.
TEMPERAMENT & CARE A hardy
fish that does well in a
community tank. Do not

combine with aggressive fish
which may nip the flowing
fins. Needs clean, well-filtered
water and regular feeds to
grow to its full potential.

BREEDING Females
produce broods of up
to 50 every month.

YUCATAN MOLLY *POECILIA VELIFERA*

DESCRIPTION A spectacular animal with a very high and long-based dorsal fin. The body is slate gray to bluish in color, becoming orange on the male's throat. Lots of color forms have been produced by hybridization. Maximum size 6 in.

DISTRIBUTION Yucatan peninsula, Mexico.

TEMPERAMENT & CARE Can be combined with other fish without any problems. For the health of these fish, it is essential that large regular partial water changes are carried out and a good filter is included in the setup.

82°f
▲
73°f

BREEDING Females produce up to 250 fry every month.

GREEN SWORDTAIL *XIPHOPHORUS HELLERI*

DESCRIPTION The commonly found wild form is green with a red stripe running through the eye to the caudal peduncle. The dorsal fin often has red or yellow in it. Males have lower rays of the caudal fin extended into a sword. Many different color forms found in the wild have hybridized in captivity. Lyretail and hi-fin forms are also known. Maximum size 4 in.

DISTRIBUTION Atlantic coastal drainages from Rio Nautla in Mexico to Belize.

TEMPERAMENT & CARE A well-behaved species, but adult males will spar with each other and may become bullies. Need a large well-planted aquarium and a mixed diet including live foods.

BREEDING Females produce up to 250 fry every month.

81°f
▲
70°f

SOUTHERN PLATY *XIPHOPHORUS MACULATUS*

DESCRIPTION A stocky-bodied fish which in the wild generally has a gray body with a few black spots on the sides or in the fins. In captivity they have been developed into hundreds of different color forms plus hi-fin, lyretail and plumetail forms as well. Maximum size 2 in.
DISTRIBUTION Atlantic coastal drainages from Rio Jamapa in Mexico southward to Belize and Guatemala.
TEMPERAMENT & CARE Peaceful community fish which fits in with most other fish.

81°f
▲
70°f

Generally hardy but will not tolerate poor water quality and dislikes salt in the water.

BREEDING Females produce broods of up to 50 every month.

VARIABLE PLATY *XIPHOPHORUS VARIATUS*

DESCRIPTION A more slender species than the southern platy which, in the wild, is often greenish with black markings and sometimes red in the fins. They have since been developed into a myriad of color forms and hi-fin, lyretail, and plumetail forms as well. Maximum size 2 in.
DISTRIBUTION From the Rio Soto La Marina system southward to the Rio Nautla in Mexico.
TEMPERAMENT & CARE An undemanding fish that will adapt to most conditions well. Eats all foods but takes up to two years to fully develop its coloration.

BREEDING Females produce broods of up to 50 every month.

75°f
▲
70°f

Rainbow Fish and Silversides

SUBORDER Atherinoidei

Rainbow fish and silversides are a group of rather

small slender fish with comparatively large eyes and two dorsal fins.

Most species are schooling fish which are only really happy

when kept in a group of six or more. They are found throughout

most oceans of the world and in brackish and freshwater habitats,

as well. The species that hobbyists have had most experience with

come from Australia, Celebes, Papua New Guinea, and Madagascar,

but there are others which have yet to make their way into aquarists'

tanks, including several genera from Mexico.

MADAGASCAN RAINBOW FISH *BEDOTIA GEAYI*

DESCRIPTION A beautiful slender-bodied fish with dark midlateral stripe. The dorsal and anal fins are yellowish orange with black edges, and the caudal fin has a black crescent toward the edge which is surrounded with creamy white. Maximum size 5 in.

DISTRIBUTION Madagascar and the surrounding islands.

TEMPERAMENT & CARE Good community fish which likes to live in a group of six or more rainbow fish. Eats all foods but prefers those which float or are in the midwater region.

Good filtration and well-oxygenated water are important to its well-being.

BREEDING Lays quite large eggs in plants near the surface.

MACCULLOCH'S RAINBOW FISH *MELANOTAENIA MACCULLOCHI*

DESCRIPTION Overlaying the silvery body color are four or more longitudinal black stripes. These are particularly strong toward the rear of the fish. The fins are orange to reddish. Males have the first dorsal fin longer and more pointed than the female. Maximum size nearly 3 in. Several different species are offered for sale in aquarium stores under this name, but these grow larger and have different coloration.

DISTRIBUTION Australia and Papua New Guinea.

TEMPERAMENT & CARE Schooling fish which does well in the aquarium. Good water quality is important, but otherwise they are hardy fish which eat anything.

BREEDING Lays eggs in plants near the surface.

FORKTAILED BLUE-EYE *Pseudomugil furcatus*

DESCRIPTION A small (almost 2 in.) rainbow fish whose males have the most beautiful coloration. All the fins have bright yellow and black on them, and the throat is a gorgeous orangy yellow. Females are much plainer and lack the throat color.

DISTRIBUTION Papua New Guinea.

TEMPERAMENT & CARE A generally peaceful species, but males will spar from time to time. Ideally keep them in a small group of one male and three females. They like some planted areas in their aquarium but plenty of open swimming areas as well.

77°f
72°f

BREEDING Lays large eggs in plants near the surface. Females only produce one or two eggs per day but spawn every day.

CELEBES RAINBOW FISH *Telmatherina ladigesi*

DESCRIPTION A semi-transparent fish with a gleaming blue stripe running along the rear half of the body. The male's second dorsal and anal fin have extended black fin rays. Otherwise the fins are pale yellow. Maximum size 2½ in.

DISTRIBUTION The island of Celebes, Indonesia.

TEMPERAMENT & CARE A shoaling fish that is always on the move. Likes clean water conditions and aeration in the tank. Will eat all foods from the surface or midwater

regions but will ignore food once it has reached the aquarium bottom.

BREEDING Spawns in fine-leafed plants at first light.

81°f
72°f

Other Bony Fishes

The superorder Teleostei (true bony fish)

contains about 10,000 or so species of freshwater fish.

However, only just over 1,000 are regularly seen in the aquarium

trade. Part of the reason for only 10 percent of bony fish being

available is that just over half of the known species either grow too

large or eat a diet that cannot be reproduced in captivity.

This still leaves at least 4,000 species which could be kept

in an aquarium. Despite this wonderful diversity of fish which

could be kept by aquarists, it is interesting to note that statistics

show that 90 percent of aquarium-fish sales are

actually of only 20 species.

PETER'S ELEPHANTNOSE *GNATHONEMUS PETERSII*

DESCRIPTION A strange-looking fish with a long elephant-like trunk which appears to have been stuck on to the head. It has a very thin, elongated caudal peduncle. The body and fins are black except for two vertical lines. Maximum size 8 in.
DISTRIBUTION Cameroon, Nigeria, and Zaire.
TEMPERAMENT & CARE Peaceful with other species but territorial toward its own. Needs a soft substrate and caves to hide in during the day. Sensitive to poor water quality.

81°f
▲
72°f

BREEDING Unknown.

FIRE EEL *MASTACEMBELUS ERYTHROTAENIA*

DESCRIPTION A long eel-like fish with dark body and fiery red stripes. The nose is movable and the nostrils inside tubes are on either side. The dorsal, caudal, and anal fins are joined into one continuous fin. Maximum size 3 ft.
DISTRIBUTION Borneo, Burma, Thailand, and Sumatra.
TEMPERAMENT & CARE This is a nocturnal predator that will eat any fish it can fit in its mouth. It likes to burrow, and the substrate should be sand or fine gravel to accommodate this habit. Feed only live foods.

BREEDING Unknown.

81°f
▲
75°f

AROWANA *OSTEOGLOSSUM BICIRRHOSUM*

DESCRIPTION A slender-bodied, silvery fish with very long-based dorsal and anal fins that almost join up with the tail. The lower jaw has a forked bony protuberance which gives the animal a very odd appearance. Maximum size 4 ft.
DISTRIBUTION Amazon.
TEMPERAMENT & CARE A large predator which will eat any fish small enough to fit in its mouth. Must have a very large tank with plenty of swimming room and some plant cover.

84°f
▲
75°f

BREEDING After spawning, the male looks after the eggs and fry in his mouth for about 55 days. The fry are 4 in. long upon release.

GREEN PUFFERFISH *TETRAODON FLUVIATILIS*

DESCRIPTION A strange-looking fish with beak-like mouth. The body is greenish yellow fading to white on the belly with large black spots. When frightened it sucks in water and puffs its body up like a balloon. Maximum size 6 in.
DISTRIBUTION Southeast Asia.
TEMPERAMENT & CARE An aggressive fish which may only be kept with bigger fish and never with its own species. Eats all live foods but loves snails which it crunches up with its beak. Add 1 teaspoonful of sea salt per gallon of water.

BREEDING Lays its eggs in a pit. The male protects them until the fry are able to take care of themselves.

81°f
▲
75°f

Picture Credits

The Goldfish Bowl, Oxford:
pp. 6, 8, 9, 15, 16, 17
(bottom), 18, 19(b), 20(b),
21–5, 26 (top), 27(b), 30, 31,
32(b), 33, 34, 36–8, 40,
41(b), 43–5, 46(t), 47–9, 51,
53, 54(b), 55, 56, 58, 60, 61,
63, 64(b), 65, 78, 79.

Derek J. Lambert: pp. 10, 11,
17(t), 19(t), 20(t), 26(b),
27(t), 29, 32(t), 39, 41(t),
46(b), 54(t), 64(t), 66, 68, 69,
70–3, 75, 76.